The Patchsmith's
ONE BLOCK MUG RUGS

by Amanda Weatherill

PATCHSMITH ONE BLOCK MUG RUGS
Text and Pattern copyright © 2016 Amanda Weatherill
Paperback Edition Published: 2016
All rights reserved.

No part of this publication may be reproduced, stored in retrieval system, copied in any form or by any means, electronic, mechanical, photocopying, recording or otherwise transmitted without prior permission in writing from the author.

The designs and projects in this book are copyright and must not be made for sale without prior permission from the author, Amanda Weatherill.

The information given in this book is presented in good faith. The author has made every effort to ensure that the instructions in this book are accurate. Please study the instructions and diagrams for the pattern you wish to make. However, no warranty is given, nor results guaranteed as responsibility cannot be taken for the choice of fabric, tools, human error or personal skill.

CONTENTS

GENERAL INSTRUCTIONS (Fabric, techniques and binding) 1

MUG RUG PATTERNS

HEART SIDEBAR 9

FLOWER SIDEBAR 13

SCALLOP SIDEBARS 17

STRIPED SIDEBARS 21

COLUMN SIDEBAR 23

STARS & STRIPES SIDEBAR 25

CHECKERBOARD SIDEBARS 27

BEEHIVE SIDEBARS 29

COURTHOUSE STEPS SIDEBAR .. 35

BIRDHOUSE SIDEBARS 37

BLOCKS

PATCHSMITH DIASY BLOCK 41

CHURN DASH BLOCK 43

PADDLES BLOCK 44

COURTHOUSE STEPS BLOCK 45

WREATH BLOCK....................................... 46

PATCHWORK STAR.................................. 47

MUG-OF-TEA BLOCK 48

About the Author.. 50

Introduction and General Instructions

What is a mug rug?

If you are not familiar with mug rugs you may be mistaken in thinking a mug rug is just a coaster. However, a mug rug is so much more – it is a mini quilt that is larger than a coaster but smaller than a placemat – it is sized to hold both a cup and a cookie or small cake plate. But these versatile little mini quilts can be used any time you require a mat or decoration for your table, shelf or dresser.

Mug rugs are quick to put together and can be made with whatever fabrics you have to hand. As such they make the perfect project when you only have an hour or two to spare or when you need a last minute gift in a hurry. Mug rugs add a pop of colour to any flat surface and are a great way to experiment with colour, pattern and technique.

Throughout this book you will find ten different designs to transform any 6" block into a functional and fun mug rug. You will also find seven 6" block designs to get you started on your mug rug making journey.

Choosing a Block

The designs in this book have been created specifically to work with any 6" quilt block. Quilt blocks are often referred to by their finished size – that is the size of the block once it is stitched into the finished quilt i.e. 4", 6", 8", 12". The 'unfinished size' is the size of the block before it is stitched in place and it will include the seam allowances. Thus a 4" block will measure 4½" square before it is stitched together and a 12" block will measure 12½" unfinished.

For all the patterns in this book you will need one 6" block (finished size) which will actually measure 6½" (unfinished size) as it will include the seam allowances. This can be any block of your choice – patchwork, appliqué or embroidery. You could even use a 6½" square of novelty fabric instead. To get you started I have provided instructions for the seven blocks used throughout this book - you will find them on pages 41-49.
Tip: *If your block doesn't quite measure 6½" you can trim many of the sidebars to fit. The appliqué sidebars are particularly good for trimming down.*

And whilst we are talking about measurements – I have listed all cutting measurements in the format width x height (*width measurement is given first and height measurement second*). This is handy to know if your fabric choice has a directional print or you are fussy cutting any pieces.

Throughout this book I have suggested that you make the appliqué sidebars before attaching them to your chosen block. This method is easier when centering the appliqué. However, if you prefer you can stitch the background sidebars to your chosen block prior to adding the appliqué – just remember to allow for the binding when placing your appliqué.
Tip: *If you are new to mug rug making you can cut your sidebars 1" wider than the measurements given and trim them to size after the appliqué has been added.*

Fabric Choices
Due to their size, mug rugs are an excellent use for some of those fabric scraps left over from a bigger project. The largest piece of fabric you will require for any of the projects in this book is 13" x 8" and that is for the backing. The appliqué detailing uses much smaller pieces – perfect for using up scraps, charm squares or recycled fabrics. I have just two requirements for my fabric: firstly it has to be 100% cotton and secondly it must be colour-fast (you can test any fabric by soaking a small piece in a bowl of water – the water should remain clear). If you stick to these two rules you will be fine.

If you are new to mug rugs or small quilts then a good way to build up a fabric stash is to use pre-cuts fabric packs. These can be found in most quilting and fabric shops. Pre-cuts come in many different sizes and the best sizes for mug rugs are charm packs (5" squares) and 'layer cakes' which are made up on 10" squares. However, it is also handy to have a few fat-quarters (quarter of a yard/metre) ready for background and backing.

As you build up confidence and discover the pleasure of creating functional mug rug mini quilts from scraps of fabric, you will automatically find yourself trying unusual fabric combinations and using darker backgrounds. But to begin with a versatile background fabric will have a small print and not be too bold in design or colour.

For small items, such as birds' beaks and small hearts, felt is a good option as it doesn't fray. Alternatively you can embroider small details.

Do not neglect the back of your mug rug. This is particularly important if you are creating the mug rug as a gift. Try to choose a backing fabric that will complement the front of the mug rug. Novelty fabrics work well or choose a fabric that co-ordinates with the mug rug.

Before you start
Fabric requirements and cutting directions are given at the beginning of each pattern and all cutting sizes include a ¼" seam allowance. You can press seams open or to one side, whichever you prefer, and it is often better to press towards the darker fabric unless stated otherwise.

Using the patterns

I would recommend that you read through all instructions for the pattern of your choice before beginning. It will help when choosing fabrics. If your chosen pattern includes appliqué you will find the appliqué templates with the pattern at the correct size. Some of the appliqué images have been reversed – you should trace them exactly as shown and they will be the right way round on your finished mug rug.

Appliqué

The patterns in this book use the quick and easy fusible method of appliqué using lightweight fusible webbing (i.e. Bondaweb, Vleisofix, Wonderweb or similar).

You will find appliqué instructions with each pattern but here they are in a little more detail:

1. Trace around the appliqué shapes onto the paper side of the fusible webbing. Fusible webbing has two sides – one smooth (paper side) and one rough (webbing side). Trace the design onto the smooth paper side.
Note: Some of the shapes have been reversed – trace them exactly as shown.

2. Cut out the shapes roughly (do not cut out accurately at this stage). You should leave approximately ¼" free around each shape when cutting out.

3. Follow the manufacturer's instructions to iron the fusible webbing cut outs onto the WRONG side of your chosen fabrics. The rough (webbing) side should be facing the WRONG side of your fabric and you will be ironing the paper side. DO NOT IRON THE WEBBING SIDE – YOU WILL RUIN YOUR IRON.

4. Allow the fabric to cool completely before cutting out the shapes accurately along the traced lines.

5. Peel the paper away from the fusible webbing/fabric.

Tip: *If you have difficulty peeling the paper away from the fabric, scratch the paper gently with a pin until you create a tear in the paper. Slide the pin between the fabric and paper. You should then be able to remove it easily.*

6. This will leave a layer of glue on the fabric cut outs. Position the fabric cut outs, with the glue side facing down, onto the RIGHT side of the mug rug. Use the appliqué

page and photo as a guide to their placement and make a note of any pieces which overlap. When happy with the arrangement, fuse the pieces in place according to manufacturer's instructions.

TIP: *Always leave enough room between the appliqué and the edge of the mug rug to allow for binding.*

7.	Finally stitch the appliqué shapes securely in place by hand or machine. You can use a running stitch, blanket stitch or any decorative stitch you prefer. It is important to stitch the pieces so that they do not come off when the mug rug is laundered.

Quilting

Mug rugs can be quilted with any thick material you have to hand – it doesn't have to be batting or wadding. You can use old towelling, wool fabric, flannel or interfacing. Whatever you use though should be washable and thick enough to protect the table from hot cups/liquid. I use both natural and synthetic materials ranging in thickness from 2 oz to 4 oz.

When it comes to quilting the finished mug rug, you can make it as simple or as complex as you like, whether by machine or by hand. You can even leave the mug rug unquilted if you wish.

To prepare your mug rug for quilting, lay the backing material with WRONG side facing up, lay the batting on top and finally lay the mug rug with RIGHT side facing up on top of both. (In effect you have a sandwich of batting between the backing material and the mug rug top.) Baste or pin all three layers together, ensuring that the backing and top remain flat and smooth. Quilt as preferred (hand or machine) and quilt around any appliqué shapes.

Tip:	*The closer your quilting is to the appliqué shape will determine how 'puffed up' the appliqué is. Try stitching very close (almost touching) and then try ⅛" away on another mug rug and see the difference.*

Once all quilting has been completed, trim the backing and batting level with the mug rug top.

Binding Methods

There are many different ways to finish your mug rugs. For all the patterns within this book I have used 1¼" wide cotton strips for binding but you could use bias binding if you prefer. I do not cut my binding on the bias unless I want a particular look i.e. a diagonal stripe. All binding is cut from ordinary quilters' cotton fabric.

You can use any binding method you are familiar with or prefer. There are some excellent tutorials on-line for machine and hand binding. I have given instructions here for simple 'single fold' and mitred binding.

Single Fold Binding

1. Cut four binding strips each measuring 2" longer than the sides of your mug rug i.e. if your mug rug is 6" x 9" cut two 8" and two 11" strips.

2. With RIGHT sides together stitch a binding strip to the top and bottom of your mug rug. Trim excess binding to match width of mug rug. Press the binding away from the mug rug.

3. Repeat with the two remaining binding strips to the sides of the mug rug. Trim excess binding to match length of mug rug. Press the binding away from the mug rug.

4. Fold the binding round to the back of the rug. Turn under ¼" on the outside edge of the binding and slip stitch the binding in place. Be careful not to stitch through to the front of the rug.

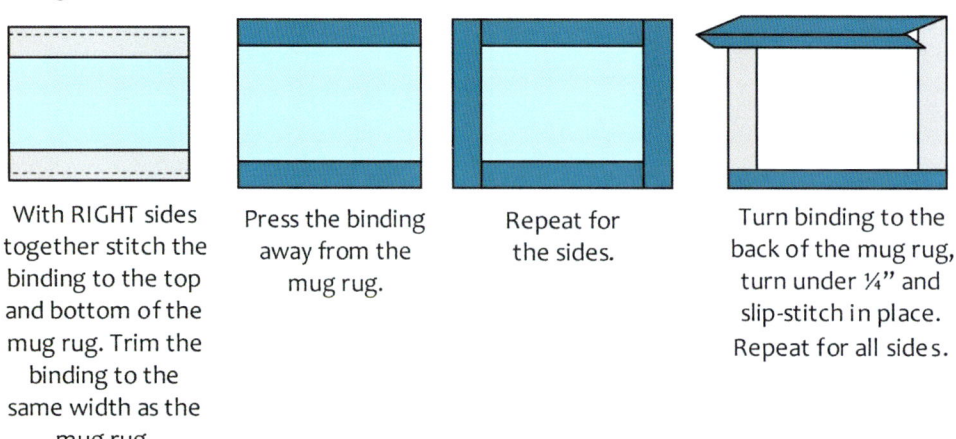

With RIGHT sides together stitch the binding to the top and bottom of the mug rug. Trim the binding to the same width as the mug rug.

Press the binding away from the mug rug.

Repeat for the sides.

Turn binding to the back of the mug rug, turn under ¼" and slip-stitch in place. Repeat for all sides.

Mitred Binding

*This method of binding creates a mitred corner finish for your mug rug.
Note: You will need one continuous length of 1¼" wide binding – this can be constructed from strips sewn together.*

1. Fold the short end of your binding strip into a triangle and align to one edge of the mug rug, RIGHT sides together, as shown (this will create a neat start/finish to your binding). Stitch the binding to the side of your mug rug but stop when you are ½" away from the first corner. Cut the thread and take the rug out of the machine.

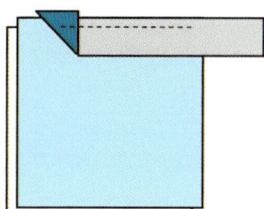

2. Now fold the binding up and away from the mug rug as shown. This will create a triangular fold in the binding at the corner.

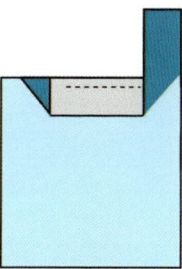

3. Hold the triangular fold (or pin it) before folding the binding down over it, aligning the edge of the binding with the side of the mug rug. Pin to secure in place. Stitch the binding along the side from top to bottom, stopping once again when you are ½" away from the next corner.

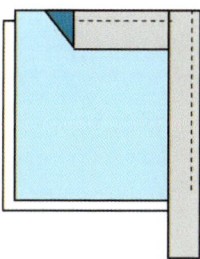

4. Repeat this process for all four corners. Continue stitching the binding until you are 1" past the beginning.

5. Fold binding to the back of the mug rug, turning under ¼" on the raw edge. Slip-stitch in place over the line of machine stitching. Make sure you do not stitch through to the front.

HEART SIDEBAR MUG RUG
(Finished size: 10½" x 6½")

Hearts signify honesty, simplicity and homely comforts.
There isn't a block that wouldn't look good next to this heart sidebar.

Fabric Requirements:

For the Background:
One 4½" x 6½" rectangle

For the Large Heart:
One 4" x 5" rectangle

For the Small Heart:
One 4" square

You will also need:
One 6" patchwork/appliqué block (6½" unfinished size)
One 6" square of fusible webbing *(i.e. Bondaweb/Wonderweb)*
One 12" x 8" rectangle cotton fabric for backing
One 12" x 8" rectangle of lightweight batting or fusible batting
1½ yards of 1¼" of binding (i.e. bias binding or cotton strips)

To make a classic Churn Dash patchwork block to accompany this sidebar follow the instructions provided on page 43.

Mug Rug Construction

1. Trace the hearts from page 11 onto the paper side of the fusible webbing. Cut out the shapes roughly - **do not** cut out accurately along the traced lines at this stage.
You do not have to layer the hearts – you could use just one large heart or two small hearts if you prefer.

2. Following the manufacturer's instructions iron the fusible webbing cut-outs onto the WRONG side of your chosen heart fabrics.

3. Allow the fabrics to cool before cutting out the hearts accurately along the traced lines. Peel off the backing paper.

4. Position the fabric hearts onto the RIGHT side of the 4½" x 6½" background rectangle ensuring you leave at least ½" between the hearts and the edge of the rectangle. When happy with the arrangement, iron to fuse in place.

5. Stitch the appliqué pieces in place by hand or machine.

6. Add any additional stitching as desired. Do not worry if your hand stitches are uneven or wonky – this will add a homespun look to your mug rug.
Tip: I added a simple running stitch around the large heart using two strands of embroidery thread. I left enough room between the embroidery and the appliqué for quilting.

7. With right sides together stitch the appliquéd rectangle to the side of your chosen patchwork/appliqué block. The mug rug top should measure 10½" x 6½".

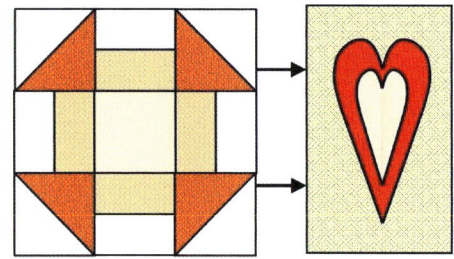

8. Lay the 12" x 8" backing rectangle, **wrong** side facing up and place the batting on top. Position the mug rug centrally on top with **right** side facing up. Baste or pin all three layers together, ensuring that the backing and top remain flat and smooth. Quilt along the seam line and around the hearts. Add any additional quilting to your chosen patchwork block as preferred.

9. Once all quilting has been completed, trim the backing and batting to the same size as the mug rug top.

10. Bind the mug rug using the binding method of your choice *(see 'Binding' in General Instructions for examples of binding methods).*
I used a 1¼" wide single-fold binding.

HEART SIDEBAR APPLIQUÉ
Trace around the solid lines
Dashed lines are additional stitching/quilting suggestions.

FLOWER SIDEBAR MUG RUG
(Finished size: 10½" x 6½")

Make it scrappy or make it co-ordinated.
Either way this cheery flower sidebar is sure to add a bloom to your chosen block.

Fabric Requirements:

For the Background:
One 4½" x 6½" rectangle

For the Flower Appliqué:
One 4" square for the petals (or five 2" squares if using scraps)
One 2" square for the flower center
One 1" x 4½" for the stem
One 3" square for the leaves

You will also need:
One 6" patchwork/appliqué block (6½" unfinished size)
One 6" square of fusible webbing *(i.e. Bondaweb/Wonderweb)*
One 12" x 8" rectangle cotton fabric for backing
One 12" x 8" rectangle of lightweight batting or fusible batting
1½ yards of 1¼" of binding (i.e. bias binding or cotton strips)
Stranded embroidery cotton (optional)

To make the Paddles patchwork block follow the instructions provided on page 44.

Mug Rug Construction

1. Trace five petals, two leaves, one stem and one flower center from page 15 onto the paper side of the fusible webbing. Cut out the shapes roughly - **do not** cut out accurately along the traced lines at this stage.

2. Following the manufacturer's instructions iron the fusible webbing cut-outs onto the WRONG side of your chosen fabrics.

3. Allow the fabrics to cool before cutting out the shapes accurately along the traced lines. Peel off the backing paper.

4. Position the stem centrally onto the RIGHT side of the 4½" x 6½" background rectangle lining up the bottom of the stem with the bottom of the rectangle. Next place the petals before placing the flower center on top as shown in the appliqué diagram.
Tip: *You may find it easier to fuse and stitch the petals in place before fusing the flower center.*
Finally tuck the two leaves slightly under the stem. All appliqué pieces should be at least ½" from the edge of the background rectangle with the exception of the bottom of the stem which should line up with the bottom of the rectangle.

5. When happy with the arrangement of the flower iron to fuse into position. Stitch all the appliqué pieces in place by hand or machine.

6. If you wish to add a simple running stitch around the flower or add any additional stitching you can do so now.

7. With right sides together stitch the appliquéd rectangle to the side of your chosen patchwork/appliqué block. Press. The mug rug top should measure 10½" x 6½".

8. Lay the 12" x 8" backing rectangle, **wrong** side facing up and place the batting on top. Position the mug rug centrally on top with **right** side facing up. Baste or pin all three layers together, ensuring that the backing and top remain flat and smooth. Quilt along the seam line and around the flower. Add any additional quilting as desired.

9. Once all quilting has been completed, trim the backing and batting to the same size as the mug rug top.

10. Bind the mug rug using the binding method of your choice *(see* 'Binding' in General Instructions for examples of binding methods). .
I used a mitred binding.

Appliqué sidesbars go well with patchwork blocks.

FLOWER SIDEBAR APPLIQUÉ
Trace around the solid lines
Dashed lines are additional stitching/quilting suggestions.

SCALLOP SIDEBARS MUG RUG
(Finished size: 9½" x 6½")

Scallop sidesbars create a fabric frame suitable for any type of block.
I have teamed them up here with the Patchsmith Daisy block
for a floral mug rug.

Fabric Requirements:

For the Sidebars' Background:
Two 2" x 6½" rectangles

For the Scallops:
Two 2" x 7" rectangles

You will also need:
One 6" patchwork/appliqué block (6½" unfinished size)
One 7" square of fusible webbing *(i.e. Bondaweb/Wonderweb)*
One 11" x 8" rectangle cotton fabric for backing
One 11" x 8" rectangle of lightweight batting or fusible batting
1½ yards of 1¼" of binding (i.e. bias binding or cotton strips)

You can find the templates and instructions to make the Patchsmith Daisy block on page 41.

Mug Rug Construction

1. With RIGHT sides together stitch the two 2" x 6½" sidebar rectangles to either side of your chosen patchwork/appliqué block. Press. The mug rug top should measure 9½" x 6½".

2. Trace the scallop border from page 19 onto the paper side of the fusible webbing. Cut out the tracings roughly - **do not** cut out accurately along the traced lines at this stage.

3. Following the manufacturer's instructions iron the fusible webbing cut-outs onto the WRONG side of your chosen fabric.

4. Allow to cool then cut out the scallop borders accurately along the traced lines. Peel the paper from each border.

5. Position the two scallops onto the side rectangles as shown so that the straight side of the scallop appliqué aligns with the side edge of the mug rug. When happy with the placement iron to fuse the scallop borders in place.

6. Stitch the scallop borders in place by hand or machine. Add any additional stitching if preferred.

7. Lay the 11" x 8" backing rectangle, **wrong** side facing up and place the batting on top. Position the mug rug centrally on top with **right** side facing up. Baste or pin all three layers together, ensuring that the backing and top remain flat and smooth. Quilt along the length of the sidebar seams. Add any further quilting as desired.
I quilted along each scalloped edge between the hand-stitching the scallop.

8. Once all quilting has been completed, trim backing and batting to the same size as the mug rug top.

9. Bind the mug rug using the binding method of your choice *(see 'Binding' in General Instructions for examples of binding methods).*
I used a 1¼" wide single-fold binding.

Scallop Sidebars turn the focus of attention onto the central block.

SCALLOP SIDEBARS APPLIQUÉ

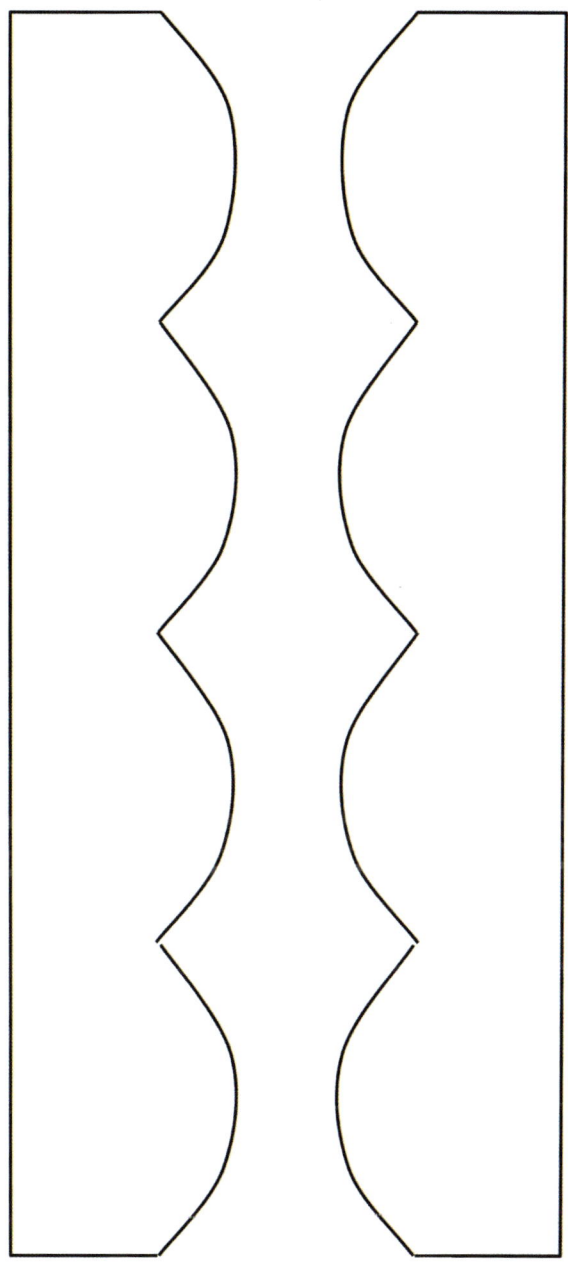

STRIPED SIDEBARS MUG RUG
(Finished size: 10" x 6½")

Striped sidebars can be created using 5" charm squares or left over binding strips. You have the option of framing your chosen block with two sidebars or one wide sidebar to create the ideal resting place for your coffee and cake.

Fabric Requirements:
For the Sidebars
Six 5" x 1½" rectangles

You will also need:
One 6" patchwork/appliqué block (6½" unfinished size)
One 12" x 8" rectangle cotton fabric for backing
One 12" x 8" rectangle of lightweight batting or fusible batting
1½ yards of 1¼" of binding (i.e. bias binding or cotton strips)

Instructions for a patchwork Churn Dash block to accompany these sidebars can be found on page 43.

Mug Rug Construction

1. Stitch the six 5" x 1½" rectangles together along the 5" length to make a 5" x 6½" unit. Press.

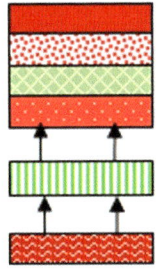

2. If you want just one sidebar trim this unit to 4" wide. If you want two sidebars, one for either side of your chosen patchwork block, cut the unit into two 2¼" strips as shown.

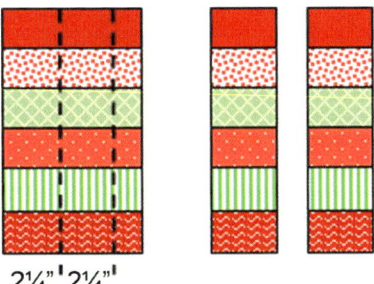

Tip: *If you prefer a smaller mug rug you can cut the sidebar strips thinner.*

3. With RIGHT sides together stitch the sidebar(s) to your chosen patchwork/appliqué block to create a mug rug measuring 10" x 6½". Press.

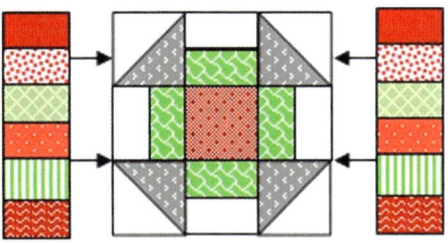

4. Lay the 12" x 8" backing rectangle, **wrong** side facing up and place the batting on top. Position the mug rug centrally on top with **right** side facing up. Baste or pin all three layers together, ensuring that the backing and top remain flat and smooth. Quilt as desired.
I quilted in-the-ditch on all seams.

5. Once all quilting has been completed, trim the backing and batting to the same size as the mug rug top.

6. Bind the mug rug using the binding method of your choice *(see* 'Binding' in General Instructions for examples of binding methods).
I used a 1¼" single fold binding.

Striped sidebars work really well with appliqué and embroidery blocks.

COLUMN SIDEBAR MUG RUG
(Finished size: 10½" x 6½")

The column sidebar provides the perfect background for adding a couple of little applique hearts, flowers or holly leaves.

Fabric Requirements:

For the Sidebar:
Two 1" x 6½" strips of cotton fabric
Three 1½" x 6½" strips of cotton fabric

You will also need:
One 6" patchwork/appliqué block (6½" unfinished size)
One 12" x 8" rectangle cotton fabric for backing
One 12" x 8" rectangle of lightweight batting or fusible batting
1½ yards of 1¼" of binding (i.e. bias binding or cotton strips)

If you wish to add appliqué to the sidebar you will need scraps of fabric and fusible webbing for each heart, flower or holly leaf.

To make a patchwork Wreath block to go with the Column sidebar follow the instructions provided on page 46.

Mug Rug Construction

1. With RIGHT sides together stitch the two 1" x 6½" strips to the three 1½" x 6½" strips along the 6½" length as shown below to create a patched sidebar measuring 4½" x 6½". Press all seams towards the darker fabric.

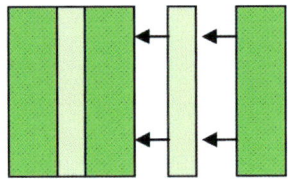

2. Stitch the sidebar to the side of your chosen patchwork/appliqué block to create a mug rug measuring 10½" x 6½". Press.

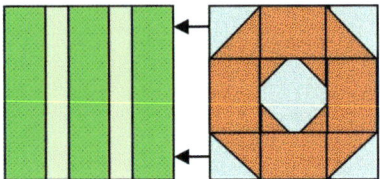

3. If you wish to add appliqué to the sidebar follow the appliqué instructions in the introduction to add flowers, hearts or holly leaves onto to sidebar or patchwork block. Ensure you leave **at least** ½" between the appliqué shapes and the edge of the mug rug.

Add holly to create a Christmas mug rug (use the small flower center for the berries).

4. Lay the 12" x 8" backing rectangle, **wrong** side facing up and place the batting on top. Position the mug rug centrally on top with **right** side facing up. Baste or pin all three layers together, ensuring that the backing and top remain flat and smooth.

5. Quilt along the seam between the sidebar and patchwork block. Add any additional quilting as desired.
I quilted in the ditch on all seams and around the flowers.

6. Once all quilting has been completed, trim the backing and batting to the same size as the mug rug top.

7. Bind the mug rug using the binding method of your choice *(see 'Binding' in General Instructions for examples of binding methods).*
I used a 1¼" wide single-fold binding.

STARS & STRIPES SIDEBAR MUG RUG
(Finished mug rug size: 9½" x 6½")

This simple patchwork sidebar will turn any block into a patriotic mug rug. Perfect for the guy in your life or as a hostess gift for those Flag Holiday barbecues.

Fabric Requirements:
For the Flag Sidebar:
- One 2" x 2¾" navy rectangle
- Two 2" x 1¼" strips of red fabric
- One 2" x 1¼" strip of cream fabric
- Two 3½" x 1¼" strips of red fabric
- Three 3½" x 1¼" strips of cream fabric

You will also need:
- One 6" patchwork/appliqué block (6½" unfinished size)
- One 11" x 8" rectangle cotton fabric for backing
- One 11" x 8" rectangle of lightweight batting or fusible batting
- 1½ yards of 1¼" of binding (i.e. bias binding or cotton strips)

To make the Mug-of-Tea appliqué block follow the instructions on page 48.

Mug Rug Construction

1. With right sides together stitch the short red and cream 2" x 1¼" strips together as shown. Press seams towards the red fabric. This patched rectangle should measure 2" x 2¾".

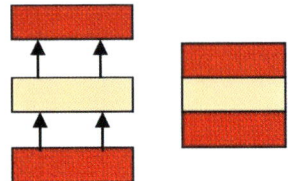

2. Repeat step 1 with the longer red and cream 3½" strips as shown below. Press seams towards the red fabric as before. This unit should measure 3½" x 4¼".

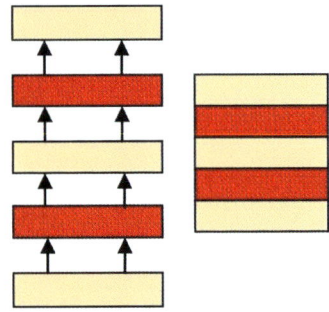

3. Stitch the two patched units and the navy rectangle together as shown to create a flag sidebar measuring 3½" x 6½". Press.

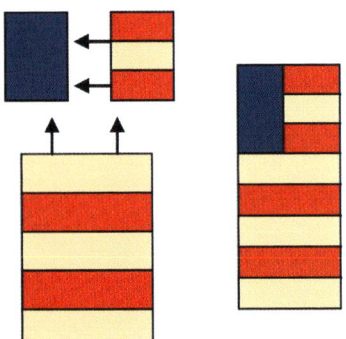

4. With right sides together stitch the flag sidebar to the left-hand side of your chosen patchwork/appliqué block. Press.

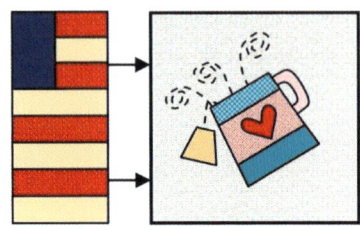

5. Lay the 11" x 8" backing rectangle, **wrong** side facing up and place the batting on top. Position the mug rug centrally on top with **right** side facing up. Baste or pin all three layers together, ensuring that the backing and top remain flat and smooth. Quilt as desired.
I quilted in the ditch around the navy rectangle before adding wavy quilting down the striped section of the Flag sidebar.

6. Once all quilting has been completed, trim the backing and batting to the same size as the mug rug top.

7. Bind the mug rug using the binding method of your choice *(see 'Binding' in General Instructions for examples of binding methods).*
I used a 1¼" wide single fold binding.

CHECKERBOARD SIDEBARS MUG RUG
(Finished size: 10½" x 6½"")

Easy strip piecing makes quick work of these patchwork sidebars. Cut half your strips from white fabric for a checkerboard look or use contrasting fabric for a stunning mug rug border.

Fabric Requirements:
For the Checkerboard Sidebars:
Six 7" x 1½" strips of two different fabrics (three of each)

You will also need:
One 6" patchwork/appliqué block (6½" unfinished size)
One 12" x 8" rectangle cotton fabric for backing
One 12" x 8" rectangle of lightweight batting or fusible batting
1½ yards of 1¼" of binding (i.e. bias binding or cotton strips)

You can find the templates and instructions to make the large Patchsmith Daisy block on page 41.

Mug Rug Construction

1. With RIGHT sides together stitch the six 7" x 1½" strips together along the 7" lengths to make a striped rectangle measuring 7" x 6½". Press seams towards the darker fabric.

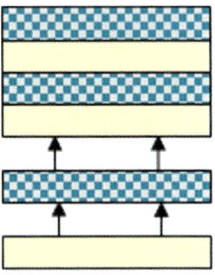

Tip: Stitch the strips all in the same direction to avoid distorting the strips. If you find you are struggling to get straight strips you can mark the seam allowance on each strip and stitch along the marked lines. Be careful not to stretch the strips when pressing.

2. From the striped rectangle cut four 1½" strips.

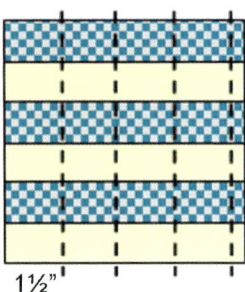

3. Stitch two strips together, flipping one of the strips upside down, to create a checkerboard sidebar measuring 2½" x 6½". Press. Repeat with the remaining two strips.

4. With right sides together stitch a sidebar to both sides of your chosen patchwork/appliqué block. Press.

Tip: Position the checkerboard sidebars so they are a mirror image of each other.

5. Lay the 12" x 8" backing rectangle, **wrong** side facing up and place the batting on top. Position the mug rug centrally on top with **right** side facing up. Baste or pin all three layers together, ensuring that the backing and top remain flat and smooth. Quilt in-the-ditch along each seam before adding any additional quilting as desired.

6. Once all quilting has been completed, trim the backing and batting to the same size as the mug rug top.

7. Bind the mug rug using the binding method of your choice *(see 'Binding' in General Instructions for examples of binding methods)*.
I used a 1¼" wide single-fold binding.

BEEHIVE SIDEBARS MUG RUG
(Finished size: 11½" x 6½")

Whether you add a single hive sidebar to a flower block or you add both the hive and bee sidebars to a patchwork block one thing is certain - this mug rug is sure to create a buzz on your table.

Fabric Requirements:

For the Sidebars Background:
Two 3" x 6½" rectangles

For the Hive:
Five 3" x 1½" strips cut from yellow fabrics

For the Patched Bees:
Three 3" x ¾" black strips
Two 3" x ¾" yellow/orange strips
(*Alternatively you can appliqué the yellow/orange stripes onto each bee body*).

You will also need:
- One 6" patchwork/appliqué block (6½" unfinished size)
- Scraps for wings and hive entrance
- One 6" square of fusible webbing (*i.e. Bondaweb/Wonderweb*)
- One 13" x 8" rectangle cotton fabric for backing
- One 13" x 8" rectangle of lightweight batting or fusible batting
- 1½ yards of 1¼" of binding (i.e. bias binding or cotton strips)
- Stranded black embroidery thread

Mug Rug Construction
Hive Sidebar

1. With right sides together stitch the five yellow 'hive' strips together along the 3" lengths to create a patched rectangle measuring 3" x 5½". Press. This patch will be used as the fabric for the hive.

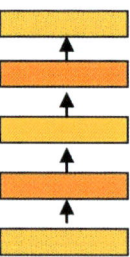

Tip: Shorten your stitch length when stitching the strips together to avoid the seams coming apart in the appliqué process.

2. Trace the hive outline from page 33 onto the paper side of the fusible webbing. Make sure you also trace at least one of the dotted lines as this will help you line up your seams and keep the hive straight. Also trace one hive door. Cut out the tracings roughly leaving ¼" around each tracing – **do not** cut out accurately along the lines at this stage.

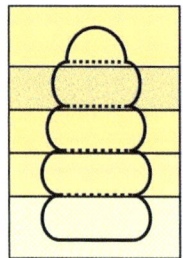

3. Position the hive onto the WRONG side of the patched unit created at step 1, lining up the dotted line on the tracing with a stitched seam on the patch. Iron the tracing in place following the manufacturer's instructions.

Tip: If you think the background may show through you can fuse a square of muslin to the WRONG side of the patched unit and treat as one piece. In this case you may not be able to see the stitched seams to match them up with the tracing so try to position the hive tracing as straight as possible but do not worry if it is a little 'wonky' – it will still look good.

4. Allow to cool before cutting out the hive accurately along the traced lines. Peel off the backing paper.
Tip: Peel back the paper carefully so you do not pull the seams apart.

5. Position the hive centrally onto one of the 3" x 6½" background rectangles with the bottom of the hive placed ¾" up from the bottom edge of the rectangle. There should be at least ½" between the side of the hive and the edges of the sidebar. The hive door lies on top of the hive. When happy with the placement, iron to fuse all pieces in place. Hand or machine stitch the shapes in place.

6. With right sides together stitch the hive sidebar to one side of your chosen patchwork/appliqué block.

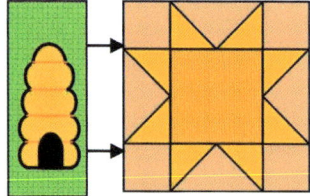

To make a patchwork Star block to accompany the Beehive sidebars follow the instructions provided on page 47.

Bee Sidebar

Instructions are given below to patch the bees. If you prefer to appliqué the two bees you can trace the dotted stripes as separate shapes and appliqué them on top of the black bee bodies.

7.   To patch the bees stitch the 3" x ¾" black strips and yellow/orange strips together as shown, to create a rectangle 3" x 1¾". Press. You will use this patched rectangle as the fabric for the bee bodies.
Tip: *Shorten your stitch length when stitching the strips together to avoid them coming apart when appliquéing.*

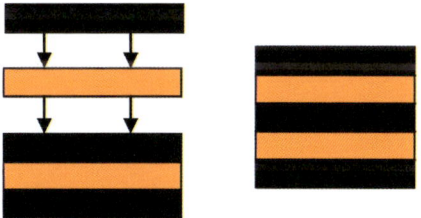

8.   Trace two bee bodies and two wings using the templates on page 33 onto the paper side of the fusible webbing. Trace the dotted lines onto the bee body tracings – this will help you line up the tracing with the striped patchwork.

9.   Cut out the shapes roughly as before - do not cut out accurately at this stage. Follow the manufacturer's instructions to iron the fusible cut-outs onto the WRONG side of the relevant fabrics. The bee bodies should be fused onto the WRONG side of the black and yellow/orange patched rectangles aligning the dotted lines with the stitched seams as best as you can.

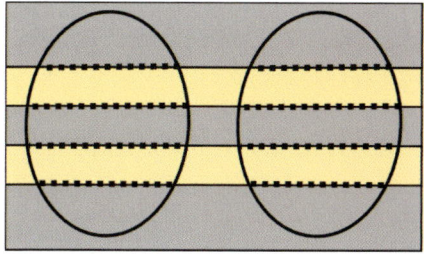

Do not worry if you can't get the seams and dotted lines to match exactly - the bees will still look good.

10.   Allow to cool before cutting out the shapes accurately along the traced lines. Peel the paper carefully away from each shape being careful not to pull the seams of the bees apart. Position the bees onto the 3" x 6½" background rectangle as indicated on the appliqué diagram. The wings lie slightly under the body. Make sure all pieces are at least ½" away from the edge of the background rectangle.

11.   When happy with the arrangement, iron to fuse the bees in place. Hand or machine stitch the bee bodies and wings in place.

12.   The bee line and antennae are created using two strands of black embroidery cotton and a simple running stitch.

13.   With right sides together stitch the Bee sidebar to one side of your chosen patchwork/appliqué block. Press.   Your mug rug should measure 9" x 6½" if using just one sidebar and 11½" x 6½" if using both sidebars.

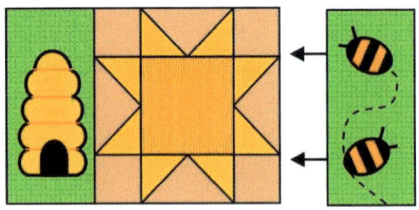

Your mug rug should measure 9" x 6½" if using just one sidebar and 11½" x 6½" if using both sidebars.
I wanted a slightly smaller mug rug so I trimmed my sidebars to 2½" wide after all the appliqué was complete.

Completing the Mug Rug
14.   Lay the 13" x 8" backing rectangle wrong side facing up and place the batting on top. Position the mug rug centrally on top with **right** side facing up. Baste or pin all three layers together, ensuring that the backing and top remain flat and smooth.

15.   Quilt around the hive and the bees. Add any additional quilting as desired.

16.   Once all quilting has been completed, press the mug rug and trim the backing and batting to the same size as the mug rug top.

17.   Bind the mug rug using the binding method of your choice *(see 'Binding' in General Instructions for examples of binding methods).*
I used a 1¼" wide mitred binding.

The Beehive sidebars work well with different size blocks as they can be trimmed slightly.

BEEHIVE SIDEBARS APPLIQUÉ
Trace around the solid lines and mark the dotted lines onto the tracing.
Dashed lines are additional stitching/quilting suggestions

COURTHOUSE STEPS MUG RUG
(Finished size: 10½" x 6½")

Courthouse Steps is a very traditional patchwork block and perfectly suited as a mug rug sidebar. It goes well with any appliqued, embroidered or a patchwork block. It will also brighten up a simple square of novelty fabric.

Fabric Requirements:

For the Center:
One 1½" x 2½" rectangle

For the Courthouse Steps:
Two 1" x 6½" strips from seven different fabrics (a total of fourteen strips are needed)

You will also need:
One 6" patchwork/appliqué block (6½" unfinished size) **or** one 6½" square of novelty fabric
One 12" x 8" rectangle cotton fabric for backing
One 12" x 8" rectangle of lightweight batting or fusible batting
1½ yards of 1¼" of binding (i.e. bias binding or cotton strips)

You can find instructions to make a Paddles patchwork block on page 44.

Mug Rug Construction
Note: Press seams away from the center throughout.

1. With right sides together stitch a 1" strip to the top and bottom of the 1½" x 2½" center rectangle. Trim the 1" strips to match the width of the block. Press. The unit should measure 1½" x 3½".

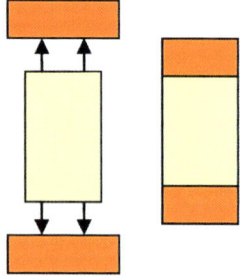

2. With right sides together stitch a 1" strip to either side of the patched unit. Trim the 1" strips to match the length of the block. Press. The unit should measure 2½" x 3½".

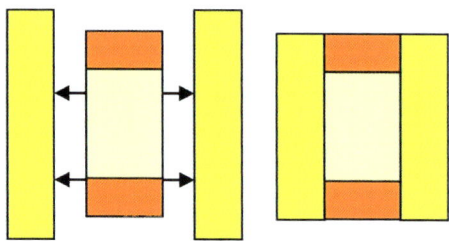

3. Continue to stitch the 1" strips to the patched unit following the order detailed in the Courthouse Steps Stitching Diagram opposite. Trim the strips and press as before. Continue until the sidebar measures 4½" x 6½".
Tip: Do not worry if your ¼" seams are not accurate just add more or less strips until your block measures 4½" x 6½".

4. With right sides together stitch the Courthouse Steps sidebar to your chosen patchwork/appliqué block to create a mug rug top measuring 10½" x 6½". Press.

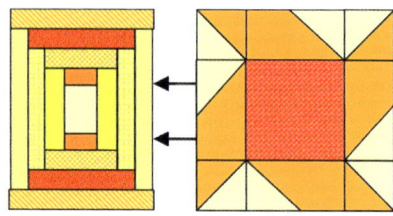

5. Lay the 12" x 8" backing rectangle wrong side facing up and place the batting on top. Position the mug rug centrally on top with **right** side facing up. Baste or pin all three layers together, ensuring that the backing and top remain flat and smooth.

6. Quilt as desired. I quilted in the ditch on all seams. However, you can make the quilting as simple or as detailed as you like.

7. Once all quilting has been completed, press the mug rug and trim the backing and batting to the same size as the mug rug top.

8. Bind the mug rug using the binding method of your choice *(see 'Binding' in General Instructions for examples of binding methods).*

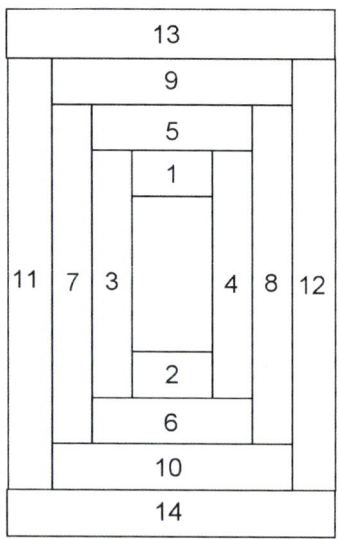

BIRDHOUSE SIDEBARS MUG RUG
(Finished size: 11½" x 6½")

Feather your nest with these delightful bird and birdhouse sidebars.

Fabric Requirements:

For the Birdhouse Sidebar:
One 3" x 6½" background rectangle
One 4½" x 3" rectangle for the birdhouse
One 3" square for the roof

For the Bird Sidebar:
Two 3" x 2½" background rectangles
One 3" x 1½" background rectangle
Two 3" x 1" strips of brown fabric

You will also need:
Scraps for the birds, wings, beaks and post
One 6" patchwork/appliqué block (6½" unfinished size)
One 6" square of fusible webbing (i.e. Bondaweb/Wonderweb)
One 13" x 8" rectangle cotton fabric for backing
One 13" x 8" rectangle of lightweight batting or fusible batting
1½ yards of 1¼" of binding (i.e. bias binding or cotton strips)

To make the patchwork Courthouse Steps block follow the instructions provided on page 45.

Mug Rug Construction

1. Patch the 'bird' sidebar by stitching the two 3" x 2½" background rectangles, the 3" x 1½" background rectangle and the two 3" x 1" branch strips together as shown. (The smaller background rectangle should be at the bottom). Press seams towards the darker fabric. This sidebar should measure 3" x 6½".

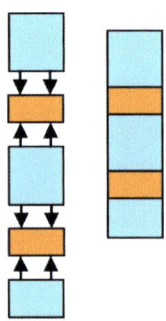

2. Trace all shapes from page 39 onto the paper side of the fusible webbing. Cut out the shapes roughly leaving at least ¼" around each tracing - **do not** cut out accurately along the traced lines at this stage.

3. Following the manufacturer's instructions iron the fusible webbing cut-outs onto the WRONG side of your chosen fabrics.
Tip: *The birds' beaks are very small so you may find it easier to use felt as it is less likely to fray. Alternatively you could embroider the beaks in place using a simple overstitch.*

4. Allow the fabrics to cool before cutting out the shapes accurately along the traced lines. Peel off the backing paper.

5. Position all pieces onto the RIGHT side of the background sidebars ensuring you leave at least ½" between the appliqué shapes and the sides of the rectangles. Align the bottom of the birdhouse post with the bottom of the 3" x 6½" background rectangle and position the top of the post so that it lies slightly under the birdhouse. The birdhouse roof lies on top. Position the birds so that they sit on the patched branches. The beaks lie slightly under the birds' bodies and the wings lie on top. When happy with the arrangement, iron to fuse in place.

6. Stitch the appliqué pieces in place by hand or machine. Add an eye to each bird using two strands of embroidery cotton and a small overstitch.

7. With right sides together stitch the sidebars to either side of your chosen patchwork/appliqué block.

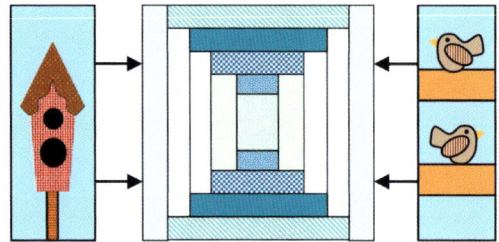

8. Lay the 13" x 8" backing rectangle, **wrong** side facing up and place the batting on top. Position the mug rug centrally on top with **right** side facing up. Baste or pin all three layers together, ensuring that the backing and top remain flat and smooth. Quilt along the seam lines and around the birds and birdhouse. Add any additional quilting to your chosen patchwork block as preferred.

9. Once all quilting has been completed, trim the backing and batting to the same size as the top. Bind the mug rug using the binding method of your choice *(see 'Binding' in General Instructions for examples of binding methods).*

BIRDHOUSE SIDEBARS APPLIQUÉ
Trace around the solid lines.
The Birdhouse post lies under the birdhouse with the roof lying on top.

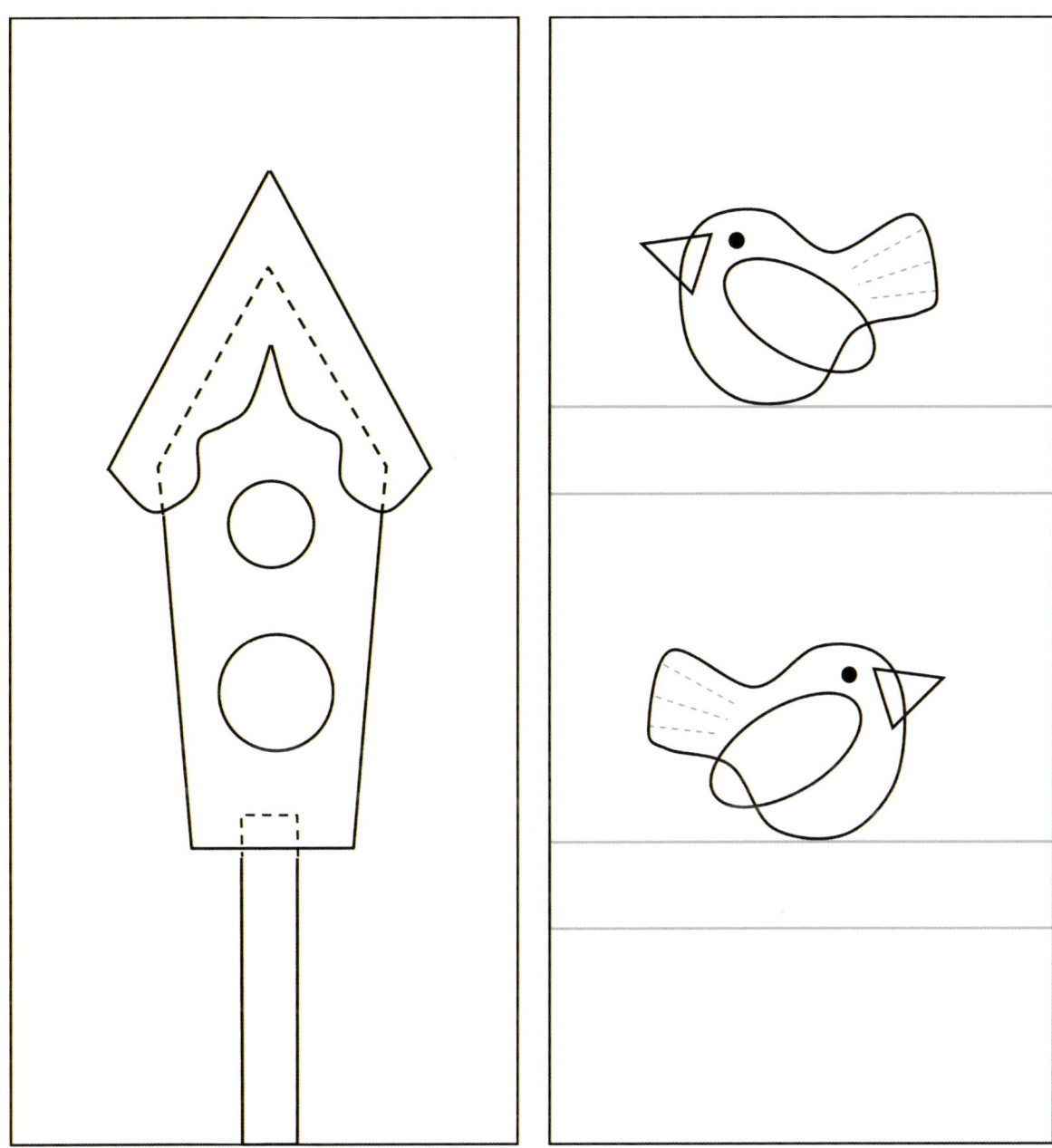

BLOCK PATTERNS

This section contains instructions for making the 6" blocks featured throughout this book. The blocks will measure 6½" square once made to include ¼" seam allowance (referred to as the 'unfinished' size). But you don't have to stick to these blocks – you can use any patchwork, appliqué or embroidery block of your choice.

PATCHSMITH DAISY BLOCK
(6" finished - 6½" unfinished)

CUTTING:
Background: One 6½" square
Four 2½" squares for corners

Daisy: One 6" square for petals
One 3" square for center

You will also need a 7" square of fusible webbing.

1. Mark a diagonal line on the back of the 2½" corner squares. This will be your stitching line.

2. With RIGHT sides together lay a marked 2½" square onto each corner of the 6½" background square. Stitch along the marked line before trimming ¼" from the stitching. Press the corner triangles open. Block should measure 6½" square.

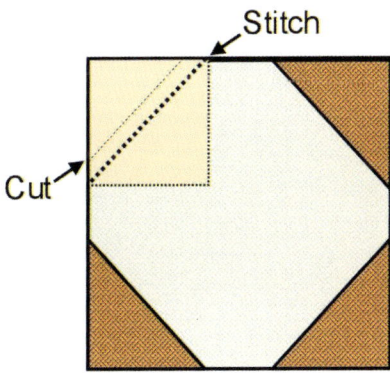

3. Trace around the flower shapes from page 42 onto the paper side of the fusible webbing. Cut out the shapes roughly - **do not** cut out accurately along the lines at this stage.

4. Following the manufacturer's instructions iron the fusible cut-outs onto the WRONG side of the relevant fabrics.

5. Allow to cool then cut out the shapes accurately along the traced lines. Peel the paper from each shape. Position the flower centrally onto the right side of the block.

6. Fuse and stitch the flower in place by hand or machine.
Tip: *You may find it quicker to stitch the petals in place first before stitching the flower middle on top.*

PATCHSMITH DAISY APPLIQUÉ
Trace around the solid lines.

CHURN DASH BLOCK
(6" finished - 6½" unfinished)

CUTTING:
Background: Four 2½" x 1½" rectangles
Two 3½" squares

Center: One 2½" square

Inner Sides: Four 2½" x 1½" rectangles

Corners: Two 3½" squares

1. Mark a diagonal line on the back of the 3½" background squares. This will be your cutting line.

2. With RIGHT sides together lay a marked background square on top of a 3½" corner square. Stitch ¼" either side of the marked line as shown. Cut along the marked line and press open to create two half-square-triangle corner units. Trim to 2½" square. Repeat to make a total of four corner units.

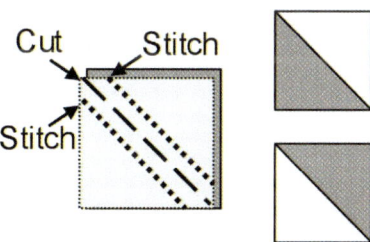

Tip: *Use the diagonal markings on your cutting mat or ruler to trim your half-square-triangles.*

3. With right sides together stitch a 2½" x 1½" inner side rectangle to a 2½" x 1½" background rectangle as shown. Press. Repeat to make four side units measuring 2½" square.

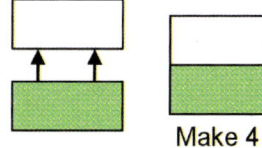
Make 4

4. Stitch a side unit to either side of the center square. Press seams towards the center square. Unit should measure 6½" x 2½".

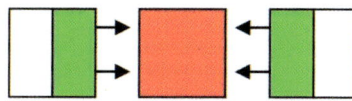

5. With RIGHT sides together stitch two corner units to either side of a side unit as shown. Press seams towards the corners. This unit should measure 6½" x 2½". Repeat with the remaining corner units and side unit.

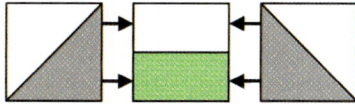

6. Finally stitch the three units together as shown. Press the seams towards the center. The Churn Dash block should measure 6½" square.

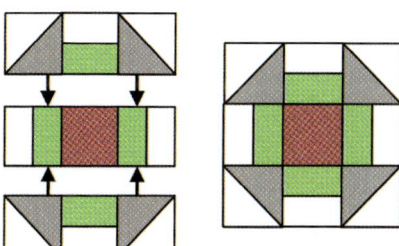

43

PADDLES BLOCK
(6" finished - 6½" unfinished)

CUTTING:
Background: Two 3" squares
Four 2" squares

Center: One 3½" square

Paddles: Four 3½" x 2" rectangles
Two 3" squares

1. Mark a diagonal line on the back of **all** background squares.

2. With RIGHT sides together lay a 3" background square on top of a 3" Paddle square. Stitch ¼" either side of the marked line as shown. Cut along the marked line and press open to create two half-square-triangle corner units. Trim to 2" square. Repeat to make a total of four corner units.

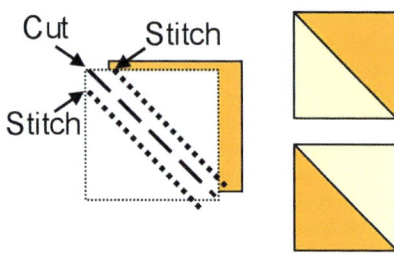

3. Lay a 2" background square onto the top right-hand corner of a 3½" x 2" Paddle rectangle as shown. Stitch along the marked line. Trim ¼" away from the stitching and press open. Repeat with the three remaining Paddle rectangles to create four paddle units.

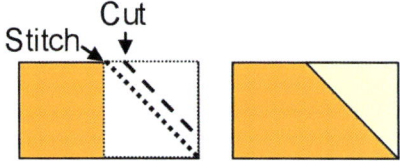

4. Stitch a paddle unit to either side of the center 3½" square. Make sure the paddles are facing in the opposite direction as shown. Press seams away from the center square.

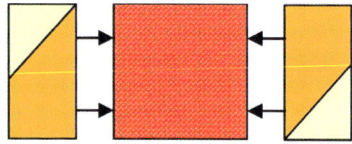

5. Stitch a corner unit to either side of the two remaining paddle units as shown. Press seams towards the middle paddle unit. These two units should each measure 6½" x 2".

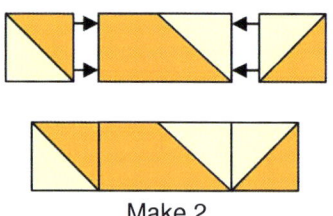

Make 2

6. Stitch the three sections together as shown. Press the seams away from the center. The Paddles block should measure 6½" square.

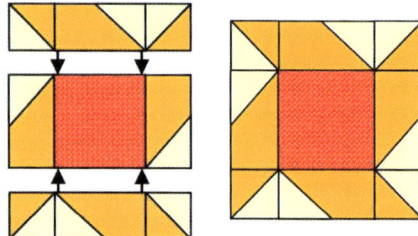

COURTHOUSE STEPS BLOCK
(6" finished - 6½" unfinished)

CUTTING:
Center: One 2" square

Steps: Twelve 1¼" x 6½" strips (two each from six different fabrics)

1. With right sides together stitch 1¼" strips to the top and bottom of the 2" center square. Trim the strips to the width of the square and press seams away from the center.

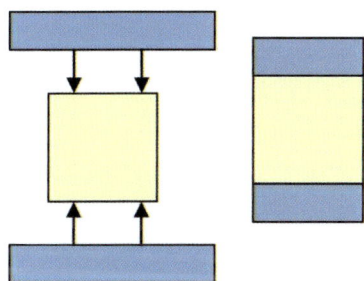

2. With right sides together stitch 1¼" strips to either side of the patched unit as shown. Trim to the length of unit and press the seams away from center as before.

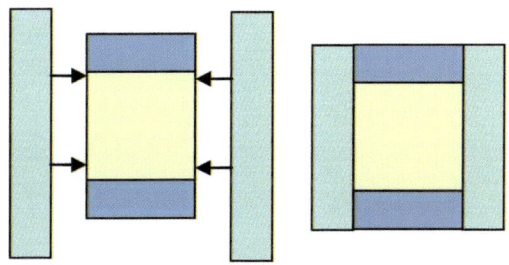

3. Continue adding 1¼" strips to the top, bottom and sides of the unit, in the order indicated by the diagram opposite, until the Courthouse Steps block measures 6½". Do not worry if your ¼" seams are not accurate – just add more or less strips to create a 6½" Courthouse Steps block, trimming the block to size if needed. Press all seams away from the center.

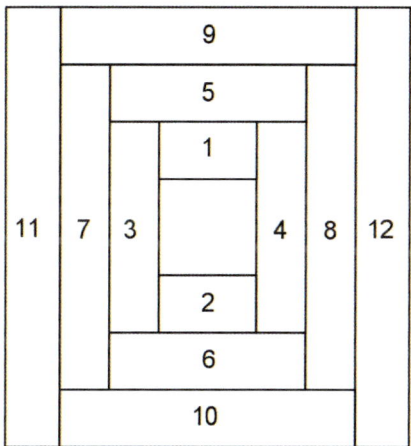

DESIGN VARIATION: Cut the 'step' strips from three different fabrics (four strips from each fabric) to create a 'boxed-in' variation.

WREATH BLOCK
(6" finished - 6½" unfinished)

CUTTING:
Background: One 3" square
Four 2" squares

Wreath: Four 1½" squares
Two 6½" x 2¼" rectangles
Two 2¼" x 3" rectangles

1. Mark a diagonal line on the back of the four 2" background squares and the four 1½" wreath squares. This will be your stitching line.

2. With RIGHT sides together stitch a 1½" wreath square onto each corner of the 3" background square as shown. Trim the corner squares ¼" away from the stitched line as shown and press open. Center unit should measure 3" square.

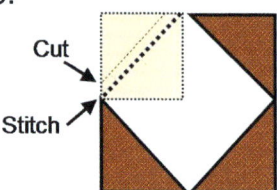

3. With RIGHT sides together stitch the two 2¼" x 3" wreath rectangles to either side of the center unit to create a middle wreath unit measuring 6½" x 3". Press seams away from the center.

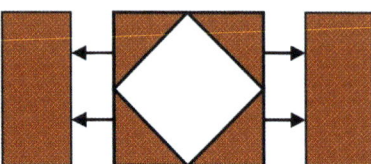

4. With RIGHT sides together lay a background 2" square onto the top two corners of a 6½" x 2¼" wreath rectangle as shown. Stitch along the marked lines before trimming as before. Press the corner triangles open. The unit should measure 6½" x 2¼". Make another for the bottom of the wreath.

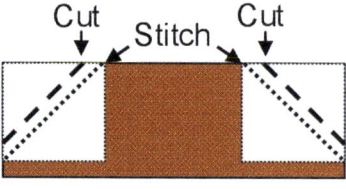

Note: *If using directional fabric for the wreath you should place the 2" background squares onto the bottom two corners of the second rectangle.*

5. Stitch the top, middle and bottom wreath units together as shown. Press the seams away from the center. The Wreath block should measure 6½" square.

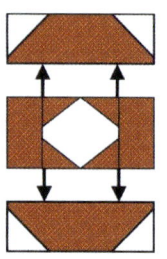 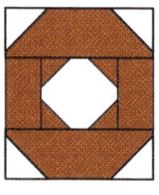

PATCHWORK STAR BLOCK
(6" finished - 6½" unfinished)

CUTTING:
Background: Four 3½" x 2" rectangles
            Four 2" squares

Star: One 3½" center square
            Eight 2" squares for star points

1. Mark a diagonal line on the back of the eight 2" star squares. This will be your stitching line.

2. With rights sides together, position a marked 2" star square on top of the left-hand side of one of the 3½" x 2" background rectangles as shown below. Stitch along the marked line. Trim ¼" away from the stitching line and press open.

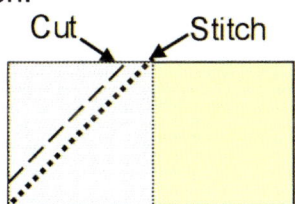

3. Repeat on the opposite corner to make one flying geese unit. The flying geese unit should measure 3½" x 2". Repeat to make four flying geese units. Note: *The triangles will overlap slightly in the middle – this will be taken up by the seam allowance when joining one section to another.*

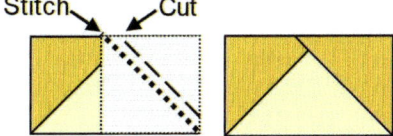

4. Stitch a flying geese unit to either side of the center square as shown. Press the seams towards the center. This unit should measure 6½" x 3½".

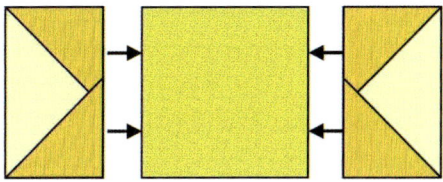

5. With right sides together stitch a background 2" square to either side of the remaining two flying geese units. Press the seams towards the corners. Each unit should measure 6½" x 2".

6. Stitch the three units together as shown, pressing the seams towards the center. The Patchwork Star block should measure 6½" square.

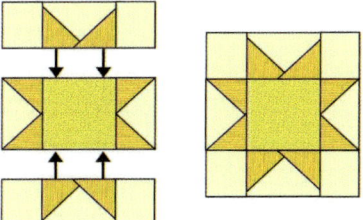

MUG-OF-TEA BLOCK
(6" finished - 6½" unfinished)

CUTTING:
Background: One 6½" square

Mug: Two 4" x 1½" rectangles
One 4" x 2" rectangle
2½" square for tea-bag
2½ square for the handle

You will also need a 6" square of fusible webbing and stranded embroidery thread if hand-quilting the steam swirls

1. To make the patched mug stitch the two 4" x 1½" rectangles to the top and bottom of the 4" x 2" rectangle as shown below. This mug unit should measure 4" x 4". Press. You will use this as the fabric for the mug appliqué.

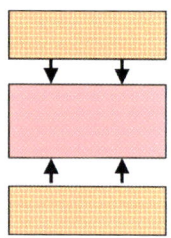

2. From page 49, trace around the mug, handle and tea bag appliqué shapes onto the paper side of the fusible webbing. Mark the position of the dotted lines onto the mug tracing. Cut out the shapes roughly - **do not** cut out accurately along the lines at this stage.

3. Following the manufacturer's instructions iron the fusible cut-outs onto the WRONG side of the relevant fabrics. (*I used felt for the tea bag.*) Position the mug cut out onto the **WRONG** side of the patched mug unit, lining up the dotted lines on the tracing with the seams on the unit as shown.

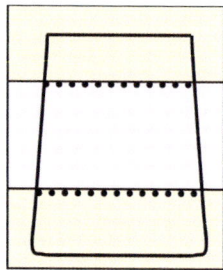

4. Allow to cool then cut out the shapes accurately along the traced lines. Peel the paper from each shape before positioning the shapes onto the background 6½" square. Ensure all pieces are at least ½" from the edge of the mug to allow for the binding.

5. Fuse and stitch all the pieces in place by hand or machine.

6. Using two strands of embroidery thread create a tea-bag string from the top of the tea bag to the mug using a simple running stitch or embroidery stitch of your choice. You can embroider the steam swirls in place now or you can quilt them when you complete the mug rug.

MUG-OF-TEA APPLIQUÉ
Trace around the solid lines of the mug, heart, teabag and handle.
Mark the dotted lines onto the mug tracing.
Dashed lines are additional stitching/quilting suggestions.

ABOUT THE AUTHOR

I am Amanda Weatherill, also known as the Patchsmith. I live in a little village nestled in the Hampshire countryside where I spend my days designing and making mini quilts - they are my hobby and my passion. My philosophy is simple – share this passion so that everybody has the opportunity to create a little piece of fabric art for their home. Mug rugs are the perfect way to achieve this. Using little more than scraps of fabric you too can enjoy the hobby of mug rug making to create something unique and functional for your desk or table. In so doing you will always have a reminder close to hand of your love of fabric, fun and colour.

Join me as I share my quick and easy designs to help you create a life full of fabric, fun and friends.

You can find the Patchsmith on Facebook, Flickr, Pinterest and Instagram.

To find out more about Patchsmith patterns and mug rug making visit
thepatchsmith.blogspot.co.uk.

Printed in Great Britain
by Amazon